D1632997

Brilliant Activities for

Grammar and Punctuation, Year 5

Activities for Developing and Reinforcing Key Language Skills

Irene Yates

Brilliant
PUBLICATIONS

This set of books is dedicated to the memory of Miss Hannah Gamage and to the children of St. Philip Neri with St. Bede's Catholic Primary School, Mansfield.

● ●

We hope you and your pupils enjoy using the ideas in this book. Brilliant Publications publishes many other books to help primary school teachers. To find out more details on all of our titles, including those listed below, please log onto our website: www.brilliantpublications.co.uk

Other books in the Brilliant Activities for Grammar and Punctuation Series

	Printed ISBN	e-pdf ISBN
Year 1	978-1-78317-125-5	978-1-78317-132-3
Year 2	978-1-78317-126-2	978-1-78317-133-0
Year 3	978-1-78317-127-9	978-1-78317-134-7
Year 4	978-1-78317-128-6	978-1-78317-135-4
Year 6	978-1-78317-130-9	978-1-78317-137-8

Brilliant Activities for Creative Writing Series

Year 1	978-0-85747-463-6
Year 2	978-0-85747-464-3
Year 3	978-0-85747-465-0
Year 4	978-0-85747-466-7
Year 5	978-0-85747-467-4
Year 6	978-0-85747-468-1

Brilliant Activities for Reading Comprehension Series

Year 1	978-1-78317-070-8
Year 2	978-1-78317-071-5
Year 3	978-1-78317-072-2
Year 4	978-1-78317-073-9
Year 5	978-1-78317-074-6
Year 6	978-1-78317-075-3

Published by Brilliant Publications
Unit 10
Sparrow Hall Farm
Edlesborough
Dunstable
Bedfordshire
LU6 2ES, UK

Email: info@brilliantpublications.co.uk
Website: www.brilliantpublications.co.uk
Tel: 01525 222292

The name Brilliant Publications and the logo are registered trademarks.

Written by Irene Yates
Illustrated by Molly Sage
Front cover illustration by Molly Sage

Contents

Introduction

The **Brilliant Activities for Grammar and Punctuation** series is designed to introduce and reinforce grammatical concepts in line with the National Curriculum Programmes of Study.

The rules of Grammar and Punctuation are not always easy to access and absorb – or even to teach. It is difficult for children to make the leap from speaking and writing to talking about speaking and writing and to think in the abstract about the words of the language. The ability or readiness to do this requires a certain way of thinking and, for the most part, repetition is the key.

The sheets for this series are all written to add to the children's understanding of these fairly abstract ideas. They aim to improve children's ability to use English effectively and accurately in their own writing and speaking.

The sheets contain oral as well as written contexts because Grammar and Punctuation are not just about writing. Sometimes the way children have learned to speak is not always grammatically correct but it is the way of speaking that they own. We always have to be aware of instances of regional or familial language and make the point that what we are teaching is what is known universally as 'correct' speech without deprecating the children's own patterns of speech.

The children should always be encouraged to discuss what it is they are learning, to ask questions and to make observations. All of this discussion will help them to understand how the English language works.

The sheets are designed to be structured but flexible so that they can be used to introduce a concept, as stand-alones or as follow-ons. The activities on the sheets can be used as templates to create lots more for practice and reinforcement purposes.

Each book aims to offer:
- groundwork for the introduction of new concepts
- a range of relevant activities
- ideas for continuation
- opportunity for reinforcement
- simple and clear definition of concepts and terms
- opportunities for assessing learning
- clear information for teachers.

Grammar and Punctuation can sometimes be a hard grind, but nothing feels so good to a teacher as a pupil, eyes shining, saying, 'Oh, I get that now!' Once they 'get' a concept they never lose it and you can watch it become functional in their writing and, hopefully, hear it become functional in their speaking.

Brilliant Activities for Grammar and Punctuation, Year 5
© Irene Yates and Brilliant Publications

Links to the curriculum

The activity sheets in this series of books will help children to develop their knowledge of Grammar and Punctuation as set out in the Programmes of Study and Appendix 2 of the 2014 National Curriculum for England.

Each book focuses on the concepts to be introduced during that relevant year. Where appropriate, content from previous years is revisited to consolidate knowledge and build on children's understanding.

Re-cap on nouns

Sort these nouns into the group that they fall into.

legs swimming

head apple skiing

rugby chocolate T-shirt toenails

beanie running shoulder gloves

bread sandwich elbow scarf socks

> Nouns that are used to name things are called 'common nouns'.

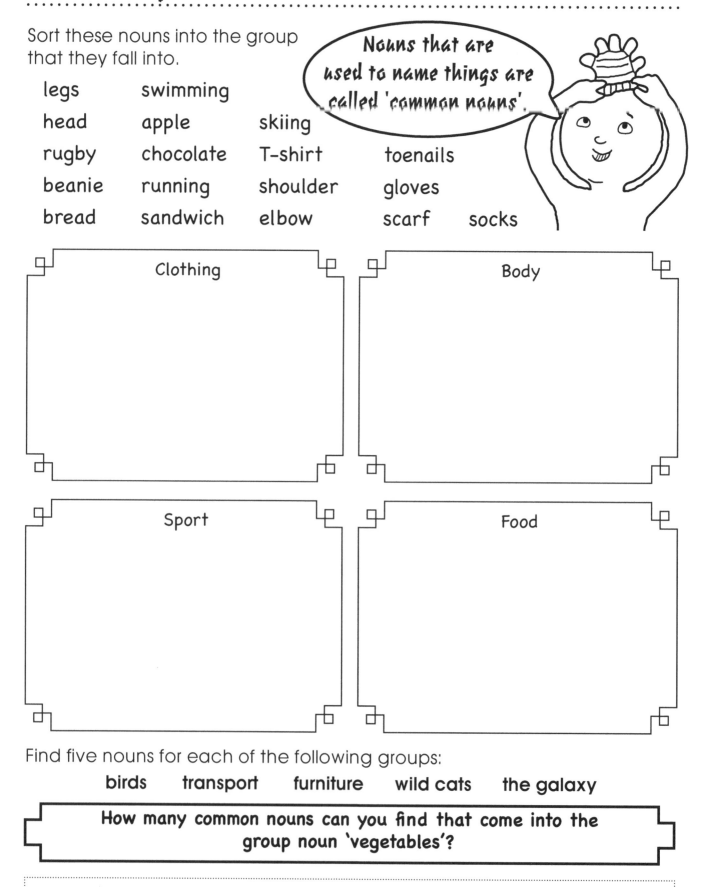

Clothing

Body

Sport

Food

Find five nouns for each of the following groups:

birds transport furniture wild cats the galaxy

How many common nouns can you find that come into the group noun 'vegetables'?

Re-cap on what a noun is. Talk about how nouns fall into categories. Get lots of verbal suggestions for groups of nouns and for the nouns that belong in them. A noun that names a group of things, ie vegetables, is called a collective noun.

Brilliant Activities for Grammar and Punctuation, Year 5
© Irene Yates and Brilliant Publications

Abstract nouns

Abstract nouns are the names we give to things we can't touch, taste, smell or see. Things like <u>ideas</u>, <u>emotions</u>, <u>feelings</u> or <u>concepts</u>.

Look at these abstract words.
How many can you use in a short story?

courage   pain   help   friendship   idea   kindness

Write your story here:

_____

_____

_____

_____

_____

_____

_____

_____

_____

_____

In groups, how many other abstract nouns can you think of?
How did you compare to the other groups in your class?

Talk through the abstract nouns and get suggestions for a storyline using as many of them as you can. Ask for more suggestions of abstract nouns.

Verbs to nouns

You can form a noun from many verbs. Here are some to show you how.

verb	noun	verb	noun
admire	admiration	move	movement
begin	beginning	permit	permission
inform	information	rebel	rebellion
laugh	laughter	serve	service

Write out the nouns for these verbs:

intend _____   persuade _____

describe _____   depart _____

Write out a paragraph that uses all four of the nouns you have formed.

_____

_____

_____

_____

_____

_____

_____

_____

_____

> **In pairs, find 10 more verbs from a book, magazine or comic and decide whether you can make nouns from them.**

Talk through and discuss. Give examples, both verbally and in written form.

Brilliant Activities for Grammar and Punctuation, Year 5
© Irene Yates and Brilliant Publications

Nouns to verbs

You can change nouns and adjectives into verbs by adding a suffix.

For example length becomes lengthen by adding an 'en'.

Take care: if a noun ends in 'i' or 'y' you will need to drop it before adding the suffix.

Use the suffixes 'ate', 'ise', 'en', 'ify' to change these words.

advert _____   captive _____

pure _____   liquid _____

central _____   hard _____

glory _____   real _____

solid _____   length _____

pollen _____   apology _____

Complete these sentences:

A person who places an advert _____

Someone who makes an apology _____

To make something pure you would _____ it.

If you place something into the centre, it is _____

Make up your own sentences with definitions.

_____

_____

_____

Find verbs for proof, hopefulness, laughter and behaviour.

Talk through with the class. Ask for lots of verbal examples before asking children to complete the sheet.

More verbs from nouns and adjectives

Write a sentence using the verb that you can get from each of the following nouns and adjectives:

decoration ⇨ _____ decorate _____

_____

invitation ⇨ _____

_____

enjoyment ⇨ _____

_____

collection ⇨ _____

_____

preparation ⇨ _____

_____

dark ⇨ _____

_____

class ⇨ _____

_____

sad ⇨ _____

_____

simple ⇨ _____

_____

action ⇨ _____

_____

> ## With a partner make up sentences using both the verbs and the noun/adjective.

Children will need to check their spellings carefully as the spelling of the root word often changes.

Brilliant Activities for Grammar and Punctuation, Year 5
© Irene Yates and Brilliant Publications

Is it a verb or a noun?

Some words can be both nouns and verbs. The spelling doesn't change but the meaning does.

Write two sentences for each of these words – one where the word is a noun and the other where the word is a verb. Like this:

Score

I always _score_ at least three goals every match. (verb)

The _score_ at half-time was 0:0. (noun)

dream _____

_____

sail _____

_____

point _____

_____

swallow _____

_____

stamp _____

_____

> **With a partner try to think of other words that can be both a verb and a noun. Use a dictionary to help you.**

Practise verbally with 'spoke', 'sound' and 'train', before pupils write their own sentences. Share in a group.

Nouns and adjectives into verbs

You can change nouns and adjectives into verbs by using suffixes, 'ate', 'ise', 'en' and 'ify'. For example:

If you give someone an <u>education</u>, you <u>educate</u> them.

Complete the following sentences:

If you make someone beautiful, you _____ them.

If you do a drama improvisation at school, you _____ .

If you make something clear to someone, you _____ it.

If someone does something to horrify you, then you are _____.

If you have deep concentration, you _____ on something.

If you give someone advice, then you _____ them.

If something is surprising, then you are _____ .

If you cool melted chocolate to make it a solid, you _____ it.

You can choose from:

solidify	improvise	surprised	clarify
horrified	advise	beautify	concentrate

Write four more sentences of your own using the root words 'ventilation', 'action', 'alien', 'dial'.

Talk about how knowing that nouns and adjectives can be changed into verbs can help their writing, by providing more variety to their sentences.

Brilliant Activities for Grammar and Punctuation, Year 5
© Irene Yates and Brilliant Publications

Verb prefix 'dis'

The prefix 'dis' changes the meaning of a verb into its opposite.

abra cad abra

You might <u>agree</u> with someone or you might <u>disagree</u> with them.

Complete the following. Choose a word from the box.

1. You might appear on stage or _____ from it.

2. You might believe what someone tells you or you might _____ them.

3. You might continue to do something or may choose to _____ .

4. Your bedroom might be well organised or it might be _____ .

| disappear |
| discontinue |
| disbelieve |
| disorganised |

Write sentences for the following to include the opposite meaning.

encourage

_____

entangle

_____

integrate

_____

interest

_____

obey

_____

orientate

_____

Use a dictionary to find more verbs that can take the prefix 'dis' and write sentences with them. Write a story using the verb 'disappear'.

Reinforce the idea that each prefix has a meaning, for example, 'dis' means the opposite, 'un' means not, 'sub' means under.

Verb prefix 'mis'

The prefix '**mis**' added to a verb usually means that the subject of the verb has done something wrong.

Instead of <u>good behaviour</u> on the trip, the whole class <u>misbehaved</u>!

Complete the following. Use the words from the box.

| misunderstand |
| mishandle |
| misinform |
| misspelt |

If you don't handle something properly,

you _____ it

If you don't understand something correctly,

you _____ it.

If you give the wrong information to someone,

you _____ them.

If you get a spelling wrong , you have _____ it.

Write sentences for these words in the same way.

judge _____

guide _____

shape _____

read _____

understand _____

lead _____

Use a dictionary to find more 'mis' verbs and write a sentence with them in. Write a story based on the word 'misunderstand'.

Reinforce the idea that each prefix has a meaning. Challenge pupils to find more words with the prefix 'mis'.

Verb prefix 're'

The prefix '**re**' usually means that the subject of the verb has got something back, or has done it again.

> The latest batch of skateboards had faults with their wheels, so they were **recalled**.

Complete these examples. Use the words from the box.

recreate
recharged
recollect
recapped

1. The class didn't understand the sums, so the teacher
    _____ the formula.

2. The battery on the phone ran out, so it had to be
    _____ .

3. The boys called on their memories to
    _____ the event.

4. The girls had loved the video, so they tried to _____ the dance moves.

Write sentences like those above for these verbs:

reactivate _____

_____

recycle_____

_____

reconditioned _____

_____

react _____

_____

redirect _____

_____

Use a dictionary to find more 're' verbs and form sentences with them. Write a story based on the word 'rebuild'.

Reinforce the idea that each prefix has a meaning. Challenge the pupils to find more words with the prefix 're'.

Verbs and nouns

Fill in the boxes.

Verb	Noun
admire	
depart	
	description
	existence
inform	
intend	
	invention
	laughter
lose	
move	
	performance
	permission
persuade	
please	
	rebellion
	service
settle	

Put the following words into the appropriate boxes:

decoration/decorate

enjoy/enjoyment

draw/drawing

proof/prove

behave/behaviour

dream/dream

Verb	Noun

┌───┐
What nouns come from the verbs 'defend', 'deliver', 'know', 'produce' and 'succeed'?
└───┘

Use other examples from texts to discuss the relationship between nouns and verbs.

Brilliant Activities for Grammar and Punctuation, Year 5
© Irene Yates and Brilliant Publications

Prefixes and suffixes

Prefixes (the bits added before the root word)
never change the part of speech. For example,
if a prefix is added to a verb, it will always
be a verb. Often they give the word
a meaning which is the opposite or
negative of the original word.

appear	<u>dis</u>appear
tie	<u>un</u>tie

Use a dictionary to find more words that begin with …

anti…	dis…	mis…	un…

Suffixes are the bits added to the end of a root word.

Find words that end with each of these suffixes:

> ## Pick five of the words you have found and use them to write a humorous piece of prose or a poem.

Recap on prefixes and suffixes. Challenge the children to call out words that begin with the prefix 'over' or 'pre' and discuss them.

Coping with clauses

A **clause** is a group of words that has a verb and a subject.

<u>**Tommy kicked the ball**</u> **that came over the fence.**

'Tommy kicked the ball' is the **main clause** of the sentence. It can make sense on its own without the rest of the sentence, 'that came over the fence' also contains a verb, <u>came</u>, but this group of words does not make sense on its own. This makes it a **subordinate clause**, one that only makes sense when it is joined to a main clause.

Draw a line to match each main clause to a subordinate clause;

Where is the skateboard   if I could go out.

This is the boy   if it doesn't stop raining.

I asked Dad   because she was reading.

The garden will be saturated   that bit the postman.

There will be no school tomorrow   Mum bought me?

Mum wouldn't come with us   that Grandad planted.

I know the dog   who lost his cat.

This is the tree   if it snows.

> **Look through sample texts, find and write out five examples of sentences with both a main clause and a subordinate clause.**

Go through a piece of text together looking at examples of main and subordinate clauses. Verbally give the children a main clause, for instance: 'we went to the park' and challenge them to offer a range of subordinate clauses.

Brilliant Activities for Grammar and Punctuation, Year 5
© Irene Yates and Brilliant Publications

More about clauses

Remember that a main clause makes sense on its own without the subordinate clause, but a subordinate clause doesn't make sense on its own.

For example, in the following sentence, you can take the subordinate clause 'who sauntered out of school' out of the sentence and it will still make sense.

The girl, who sauntered out of school, missed her bus.

Write out the main clause in each sentence.

Because it was the middle of winter the weather was freezing.

_____

The boys played cricket even though it was very hot.

_____

I can't come out until I've cleaned my room.

_____

The dog kept barking until its owner came to take it for a walk.

_____

The trees we scrumped the apples from were my grandma's.

_____

Josh couldn't play football because he'd left his boots at home.

_____

Before you cross a busy road look both ways.

_____

The bus driver had no idea where I needed to go.

_____

Write a series of main clauses to build into sentences with subordinate clauses added. Discuss before writing.

Look for main clauses and subordinate clauses in texts. Challenge children to find alternative subordinate clauses to go with the main clauses.

Relative clauses

Relative clauses are a kind of subordinate clause which uses a relative pronoun such as; **who, which, where, when, whose** and **that,** instead of repeating the noun.

Example:

That's the boy **who** lives next door to me.

Relative pronouns introduce relative clauses which tell us more about people and things.

Here's a relative clause to start a story. Continue writing it. Try to use lots of relative clauses.

The alien aircraft that landed in the playground was full of ...

_____

_____

_____

_____

_____

_____

_____

_____

Swap some ideas about how the story might progress.

Make up several relative clauses together, using the pronouns ' who', 'which', 'where', 'when', 'whose' and 'that'.

Brilliant Activities for Grammar and Punctuation, Year 5
© Irene Yates and Brilliant Publications

Looking at paragraphs

A paragraph is not just a block of sentences strung together without any thought. It's a bit like a brick in a wall. If the wall is the story, each paragraph works with the others to build the story into a good read.

Every paragraph has a main idea.

Suppose you are going to write a story entitled 'My holiday on the Moon'. Write down as many different ideas as you can. Each of these ideas could give you a idea for a paragraph. You might choose an idea from here:

How would I get there?

Moonbaby ☐

Sonic flight ○

Moonhopper

Moonscope

Purple Sea-fishing for Moonbass

Moonmobile or Moonbuggy

In groups, collaborate to produce a collage of a Moon Monster.

Have lots of discussion about various factors: travel, location, inhabitants and activities etc. Discuss the order of the paragraphs. What should the first and last paragraphs be about?

Getting cohesion into paragraphs

A paragraph has to have cohesion. This means that your sentences should flow together and make sense. You could write:

The Moon holiday was brilliant. I was so worn out when we got home. I'm glad we went. I loved the moonbabies and the moon hoppers. I got a great moon-tan.

But it would read better if you joined your ideas together like this:

Even though I was worn out when we got home I'm so glad we went on that brilliant Moon holiday. I got a great moon-tan and I loved the moonbabies and moon hoppers.

Write the next paragraph to this story in a cohesive way.

Let me tell you about ...

_____

_____

What was the first animal in space?

_____

_____

The cow that jumped over the moon! Ha ha.

_____

_____

_____

_____

┌───┐
Talk with your partner before you write down what your next paragraph should be about.
└───┘

Remind pupils that each paragraph needs to have a main idea/subject. Model writing a paragraph, demonstrating the devices you use to link sentences together.

Brilliant Activities for Grammar and Punctuation, Year 5
© Irene Yates and Brilliant Publications

Ordering paragraphs

Once you have a group of ideas for paragraphs, you need to get them in order. You don't want your reader to have to jump about all over the place.

One way to order your paragraphs is to put them in **chronological order**, that is, the sequence of events in the order that they happen.

Other ways could be by:
- Location, if you are writing about a visit
- People
- Emotions

Look at the paragraph ideas you came up with for 'A holiday on the Moon'. Now put them into some kind of order here:

_____

_____

_____

_____

_____

_____

_____

_____

_____

_____

_____

_____

Talk with your partner about your plan. Do your paragraphs flow together in a sensible way?

Explain that the order might change as you write the story, but it's a good idea to have an initial plan. Children could write their 'Holiday on the Moon' story.

Bridging paragraphs

To help your writing flow, each paragraph should have some kind of bridge to the next one.

How do you build the bridges? You make your story flow by linking the content and the text in some way. You can do it with words like:

   then   after   later   immediately

or you can do it by introducing something at the end of one paragraph and then starting the next paragraph by writing about it, for example;

   ... what should come round the corner but a moon hopper!

   The moon hopper was ...

Look again at a story or piece of text you have written. How could you link the paragraphs together better? Write your ideas here.

_____

_____

_____

_____

_____

_____

_____

_____

Share verbal thoughts with a partner; choose random ideas to end one paragraph and to start the next.

Make a display of endings and beginnings, clearly showing the bridges. Don't forget you can use a question mark at the end of one paragraph and answer it in the next one. Who was it? It was ... . Remind pupils to use bridges in their writing.

Brilliant Activities for Grammar and Punctuation, Year 5
© Irene Yates and Brilliant Publications

Brackets

Brackets ( ) are used in pairs around words to keep them separate from the rest of the sentence. If you take the words in brackets out of the sentence, the sentence still makes sense.

There was no one in town (it was Christmas Day) and all the shops were shut.

There was no one in town and all the shops were shut.

Put brackets around the words that need them in the following sentences.

Harrif invited his friends there were six of them to tea.

Lucy went with Anna her best friend and Henry's sister.

They had a lot of stuff to carry drinks, cards, presents and a cake.

The bus went the long way round there was a flood and they were late.

A bracket is sometimes called a parenthesis (plural: parentheses)

Make up three more sentences of your own using brackets.

_____

_____

_____

Make up four sentences verbally together before writing them down.

Explain that the word 'parentheses' means brackets. Words can be in brackets or, in 'parentheses'. Which word do they like best? Sometimes 'parenthesis' is used to describe the word or phrase that has been added to the sentence, rather than the brackets themselves.

Double dashes

There are two kinds of dash – single dashes and double dashes. Sometimes a pair can be used instead of brackets. Like this:

Wake up early – set your alarm – so that we can leave on time.

or

Wake up early (set your alarm) so that we can leave on time.

Use double dashes to rewrite these sentences.

The moon-jumping competition it was going to be great would start at sundown.

Does anybody know when or where it's going to end?

We might need warm things clothes, waterproofs, trainers to get it really going.

Write three more sentences of your own to carry on with the story.

_____

_____

_____

_____

_____

_____

Can you chat in such a way that you would need double dashes if you were to write down your conversation? Try it.

Do some 'whole-class double-dash' gathering through some shared texts. They might be few and far between, so reward the spotters! Point out that double dashes are not used at the end of sentences, they should use brackets instead.

Brilliant Activities for Grammar and Punctuation, Year 5
© Irene Yates and Brilliant Publications

Single dash

A single dash is used to show a pause or a change of idea/direction in a sentence - like this:

Tyrannosaurus Rex is supposed to be quite big – I've never seen one.

Tom said he's seen a dinosaur – I don't believe him!

Write some more single dash sentences, continuing the dinosaur theme.

_____

_____

_____

_____

_____

_____

_____

Work out a list of dinosaurs together – then find a way to use a dash when describing them.

Discuss the difference between dashes and hyphens – dashes look the same but a hyphen has a completely different job to do.

Lots of talking

We know that direct speech is the exact words someone says and indirect speech is speech that's reported.

"I'm going to watch the match," said Henry.
His mum told him he had better clean his room first.

Rewrite this mini-story – swapping direct speech for indirect speech and vice versa.

Henry groaned. "But it starts in half an hour!"

"Tough!" said Mum, "You'll miss the first half if you don't get a move on."

Henry surveyed the mess in his room. He said he would do it when he got back after the match.

"Not good enough" said Mum. "I know you. You'll forget or not bother at all!"

"How can I forget?" Henry said. "You won't let me!"

Mum said no she wouldn't either. She would nag him till it was done and he wasn't going to get away with it whatever happened.

"It'll be fine," Henry said and he rushed out before she could stop him, whispering nag, nag, nag, under his breath.

> ## Make up a dialogue together. Write it down. Then change it into reported speech.

'Reported' and 'indirect' speech mean the same thing. Explaining it as 'reported' might give the pupils more understanding.

Brilliant Activities for Grammar and Punctuation, Year 5
© Irene Yates and Brilliant Publications

Hyphens

Hyphens look exactly the same as a single dash, but they can join two words together, making compound words. They can make sense of phrases that might be ambiguous. Like these:

a man eating tiger would be a man eating a tiger.

a man-eating tiger would be a tiger eating a man.

a cat eating mouse would be a cat eating a mouse.

a cat-eating mouse would be a mouse eating a cat.

When you use a hyphen in this way, you make a **compound word.**

Make up some more jokey hyphenated compound words. Draw pictures.

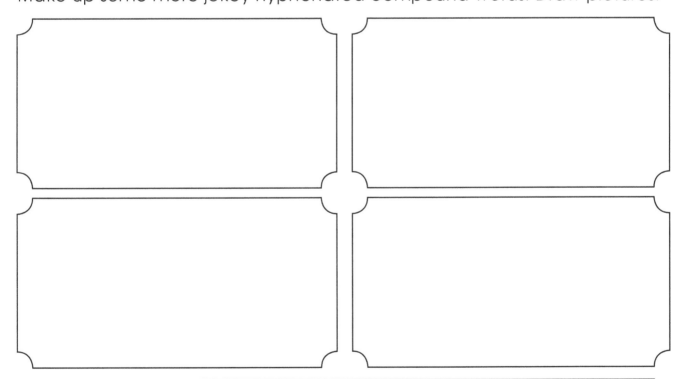

Make up jokey hyphenated words together before you write and draw them.

Focus on what differentiates a hyphen from a dash.

Anagrams

An anagram is a word or a phrase that you can form out of the letters of another word or phrase, like this:

act = cat   fries = fires
bare = bear   break = baker

Scramble these words to make new ones (some words can make more than one).

flees = _____

glare = _____   hoses = _____

layer = _____   friend = _____

licks = _____   fringe = _____

items = _____   grease = _____

reprint =_____   expect = _____

Use a thesaurus to find 12 words you can use for anagrams here and test a friend.

_____   _____

_____   _____

_____   _____

_____   _____

_____   _____

_____   _____

> **Can you write a anagram of a phrase? For example: 'rats and mice' is an anagram of 'in cat's dream'.**

Make sure the children understand they have to use the exact number of letters and use each one once only.

Brilliant Activities for Grammar and Punctuation, Year 5
© Irene Yates and Brilliant Publications

What's a phrase?

A **phrase** is a group of words that doesn't make sense on its own. We add phrases to sentences to make them more interesting.

The cat jumped in a frightened manner.

in a frightened manner is the phrase.

Here are some phrases – turn them into sentences.

1. during the afternoon
2. with fear and trembling
3. before the snow
4. for a split second
5. in the background
6. without hurrying
7. in the classroom
8. at the back

_____

_____

_____

_____

_____

_____

_____

One partner gives a short sentence. The other has to add a phrase to make it more interesting. Swap.

Photocopy a familiar story and have the children circle the phrases that they find.

Add a phrase

You can add phrases to sentences to make them more interesting.

We had a great party. (sentence)
We had a great party <u>after the harvest festival</u> (sentence with a phrase)

Add phrases to these sentences.

1. We packed our stuff.
2. I fed the puppy.
3. The crocodile snapped.
4. Dad came home.
5. I switched on the TV.
6. The park opened.
7. The tortoise crawled.
8. We slept late.

The phrase might go at the beginning or the end of the sentence.

What do crocodiles call human children?

Appetisers! Ha ha.

With a partner take one of the short sentences above and think of as many different phrases you can add to it as you can.

Take examples from the children verbally. Ask for volunteers to say something that has happened to them and get the group to decide which bits of their sentences are phrases.

Phrases that describe

Some phrases do the work of adjectives. They describe or add meaning to a noun, like this:

The boy <u>in the cool hat</u> is my brother.
The dog <u>with the waggly tail</u> is mine.

These are known as **adjectival phrases**.

Find the adjectival phrase in these sentences and underline it.

The cat with the long fur is mine.

The man with the brown shoes is a teacher.

The sail on the windmill was broken.

The house on the corner belongs to my gran.

The girl with the skipping rope is my best friend.

The alien on the bus is unhappy.

Write a sentence around each of these adjectival phrases.

_____ with huge wings _____

_____ playing football _____

_____ at the edge of the cliff _____

_____ at the end of the street _____

_____ with the tall foxgloves _____

_____ in the town centre _____

With your partner talk about what each of the adjectival phrases above could be describing before you write your sentences.

Make sure the children understand which word is the noun that the phrase describes. You could point out that although some of the phrases have verbs (eg playing football), they are phrases as they don't make sense on their own.

Phrases that do the job of an adverb

Some phrases do the job of an adverb. They tell you how, when or where an action happens.

We walked <u>into the hall</u>.
↑　　　↑　　　↑
subject　verb　adverbial phrase

These are known as adverbial phrases.

Find the adverbial phrases in these sentences and underline them.

We're going on holiday next weekend.

The alien came here three weeks ago.

The artist painted with great care.

We put all the toys in the toybox.

She read the story aloud in a very happy way.

The cat had a poor bird in its mouth.

After a while we set out for the park.

We watched TV with the sound off.

Put the adverbial phrases you have underlined in the correct box.

How	When	Where

With a partner think of other adverbial phrases that would fit into the above sentences.

Discuss with the children whether the adverbial phrases tell you how, when or where the actions happen.

Brilliant Activities for Grammar and Punctuation, Year 5
© Irene Yates and Brilliant Publications

More adverbial phrases

Remember that an adverbial phrase:
1. does the job of an adverb
2. tells you how, when and where.

Complete each of these sentences with an adverbial phrase, using the word in the brackets to help you.

There were about ten tigers (where?)

_____

Last weekend we all went (where?)

_____

The boy on the bike cycled (how?)

_____

A child ran (where?)

_____

The teacher spoke to me (how?)

_____

We got to town (when?)

_____

There was an alarm (when?)

_____

We had a fabulous day (where?)

_____

Look for more adverbial phrases in books, magazines and comics.

Use a common text to locate and discuss some adverbial phrases.

Modal verbs

Sometimes sentences contain two verbs side by side. The first is a modal verb.

I <u>must</u> be home by 8 o'clock.

↑
modal verb

Josh <u>may</u> stay until the end of the party.

↑
modal verb

Modal verbs can be used to show:

- ability: **can, could** (Jack <u>can</u> sing.)

- permission: **may, can, could** (You <u>may</u> have another piece of cake.)

- possibility: **might, shall, will** (It <u>might</u> snow tomorrow.)

- obligation: **must, should, ought** (You <u>must</u> clean your room.)

Look at the following sentences and insert a modal verb that works within the sentence.

1. When I'm bigger, I _____ be able to reach the highest branch.

2. "I _____ love to come to your party," Marie told Ayla.

3. I _____ ask my mother if she will let me.

4. "Yes, you _____ go out to play," mum said.

5. Cinderella said, "I _____ go to the ball!"

6. Jemma didn't know if she _____ be able to come.

7. Ben thought the answer to the maths problem _____ be 52.

8. Ahmed _____ climb up the rope ladder.

Make up two more sentences of your own using modal verbs. Underline the modal verbs.

> ### Say a sentence with a modal verb to your partner. Can they identify the modal verb? Swap.

Emphasise that modal verbs always appear with another verb.

Brilliant Activities for Grammar and Punctuation, Year 5
© Irene Yates and Brilliant Publications

Adjective quiz

Join these adjectives up so that they have opposite meanings.

shallow	fresh
fake	wise
stale	deep
dangerous	boring
foolish	true
brave	safe
rich	timid
exciting	poor

Think of a noun that each pair of adjectives fits and write a sentence using one of the words appropriately. The first one is done for you.

fresh/stale: The bread we had to eat was fresh.

_____

_____

_____

_____

_____

_____

_____

_____

Can you think of 10 more adjectives and their opposites? Work with a partner, you have five minutes.

Remind the children that describing adjectives are used to describe a noun or pronoun.

How to use number adjectives

When numbers are used to show the number of things in a sentence we call them **number adjectives**.

Write out a sentence for each of the number adjectives below. The first one has been done for you.

thirteen: There are thirteen cakes in a baker's dozen.

two: _____

five: _____

ten: _____

twenty: _____

one hundred: _____

two thousand: _____

Number adjectives can also show the numerical order of things, for example, first, second, third, fourth and fifth etc.

Write a sentence for each of these:

first: _____

second: _____

third: _____

fourth: _____

fifteenth: _____

one hundredth: _____

Discuss times and events of races/competitions, what position did you finish?

Look for examples in reference books and share.

Brilliant Activities for Grammar and Punctuation, Year 5
© Irene Yates and Brilliant Publications

Making adjectives

Make an adjective from each of
these nouns and write a phrase for
each of them like this:

sleep   a sleepy dog
↑   ↑
noun   adjective

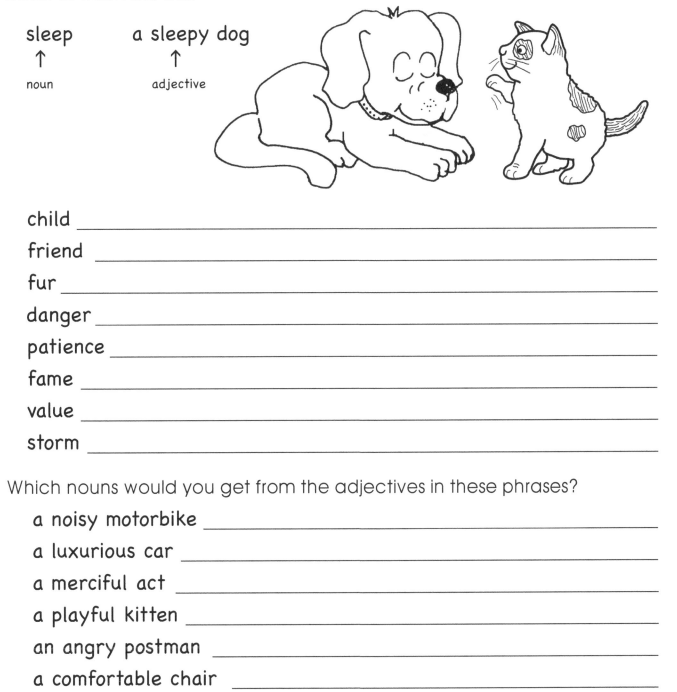

child _____

friend _____

fur _____

danger _____

patience _____

fame _____

value _____

storm _____

Which nouns would you get from the adjectives in these phrases?

a noisy motorbike _____

a luxurious car _____

a merciful act _____

a playful kitten _____

an angry postman _____

a comfortable chair _____

> **Together, choose ten adjectives from a piece of text and see if you
> can get nouns from them.**

Recap the concepts of adjective and noun.

Proper adjectives

You've heard of 'proper nouns' which start with a capital letter. **Proper adjectives** do too. They are formed from the nouns like this:

Gram waves a <u>Welsh</u> flag
The proper noun is <u>Wales</u>.

Remember the capital letter.

Decide which is the **proper adjective** for each of these proper nouns.

China _____   Mexico _____

Switzerland _____   France _____

Scotland _____   Japan _____

America _____   Greece _____

What are the proper nouns for these proper adjectives?

Turkish _____

Dutch (be careful)_____

German _____

Irish _____

Swedish _____

Egyptian _____

Spanish _____

Italian _____

Norwegian _____

> **How many countries or nationalities can you think of together that are not on this page?**

Follow this up by researching flags and nations of the world and making a display.

Brilliant Activities for Grammar and Punctuation, Year 5
© Irene Yates and Brilliant Publications

Comparative adjectives

Adjectives can change the way words are formed to show comparison.
sweet   sweeter   sweetest

These stages are called the **positive degree**, the **comparative degree** and the **superlative degree**.

Positive	Comparative	Superlative
muddy	muddier	muddiest
old		
	younger	
		shortest
cold		
	smaller	
		safest
large		
	wiser	
		bravest

Some words don't always fit this pattern as you can see below.

Positive	Comparative	Superlative
good	better	best
bad	worse	worst

Now try these:

Positive	Comparative	Superlative
beautiful		
	more delicious	
		most honest
sorrowful		
	more reliable	

Go through the concept of positive, comparative and superlative text, so that the children understand the degrees of comparison.

Similes

A **simile** is a 'figure of speech' that compares one thing to another. It is a straightforward comparison, using the word 'like' or 'as':

> **as cold as ice**
> **the wind howled like a banshee**

Make up some similes of your own and put them into sentences using these adjectives.

busy	**gentle**	**playful**	**quick**	**sharp**
tall	**pale**	**noisy**	**light**	**slow**

_____

_____

_____

_____

_____

_____

_____

_____

_____

_____

_____

_____

_____

Together work out the similes verbally and then write the sentences individually.

Go through the concept of simile. Look for similes in shared texts. Talk about the frequently used similes becoming clichés.

Brilliant Activities for Grammar and Punctuation, Year 5
© Irene Yates and Brilliant Publications

Homophones

Homophones are words that sound the same but are spelt and mean something different. Like this:

mail   male   deer   dear

Find, with the help of a thesaurus, homophones for these words.

find   _____

bawl   _____

week   _____

which   _____

guest   _____

hair   _____

pier   _____

pore   _____

which witch?

Write a sentence for each set of homophones using both words; make it funny.

_____

_____

_____

_____

_____

_____

_____

How many more homophones can you think of together in five minutes?

Have the children create a display board of homophone cartoons, using words such as knit/nit, eye/I, bare/bear, pair/pear, sun/son, break/brake, blew/blue – and lots more that the children can think of.

Apostrophes showing contractions

What do these contractions mean?

hasn't _____   we'll _____

we've _____   can't _____

o'clock _____   'tis _____

didn't _____   wouldn't _____

Write out these as contractions:

I am _____   you have _____

I have _____   who is _____

I shall _____   it is _____

could not _____   were not _____

Put the apostrophes in this paragraph.

Well go to the park. Its bound to be sunny and itll be fun on the climbing equipment. Youll need your trainers and maybe some water. Or well go to the cafe and theyll serve us some delicious ice-cream!

Can you think of any more contractions?

Photocopy a shared text for the children to read aloud together, marking all the contractions they come to. Point out that the contraction ''tis' for 'it is' is old fashioned and not in common use now.

Apostrophes showing possession

Apostrophes show possession
in nouns. For example:

the dog's kennel
(one dog, one kennel)

the dogs' kennel
(more than one dog, one kennel).

Rewrite these phrases using apostrophes.

the ears of the dog _____

the sheep of the farmer _____

the boots of the boy _____

the tail of the tiger _____

the tails of the cats _____

the books of the library _____

the bedrooms of the sisters _____

the hands of the clock _____

Make up some sentences, using apostrophes for possession, using the words:

alien _____

elephant _____

children (be careful) _____

eagles _____

cities _____

spider _____

> **Write five sentences showing possession, but leave out the apostrophes. Swap papers with a friend and get them to add in the apostrophes. Did they put them in the correct place?**

Go through all the rules for apostrophes showing possession, both for single and plural nouns. Make sure the children understand what happens when the noun is already a plural form, eg children's, people's etc.

Commas

Sometimes you can use commas instead of brackets or double dashes to separate a phrase from the rest of the sentence, like this:

London, the capital of England, is a sprawling city.

Add in the commas to each sentence to indicate the position of the phrase.

For my birthday on the tenth I want all of my friends to come to tea.

The puppy the one with the waggly tail might be coming home with us.

My friend Rashid according to his gran is the nicest boy ever.

Ian the best writer in the class won the first prize for his story.

Write four sentences of your own that contain a phrase (not a clause) separated by commas.

1. _____

_____

2. _____

_____

3. _____

_____

4. _____

_____

> **Say a short sentence to your partner, who then has to add a phrase to the sentence. Then, like 'Chinese Whispers', see how many more phrases each of you can add.**

Recap all the uses of commas that the children know. Recap the use of double dashes and brackets.

Brilliant Activities for Grammar and Punctuation, Year 5
© Irene Yates and Brilliant Publications

Parts of speech

How many 'parts of speech' do you know, recognise and understand?
Write what you know about each of these – imagine you are explaining
them to a visitor from another planet.

Nouns _____

_____

_____

Verbs _____

_____

_____

Adjectives _____

_____

_____

Adverbs _____

_____

_____

Articles _____

_____

_____

Prepositions _____

_____

_____

Pronouns _____

_____

_____

Conjunctions _____

_____

_____

Punctuation

Imagine you are explaining these types of punctuation marks to an extra-terrestrial friend. Explain what each one does as clearly as possible.

Capital letters: _____

_____

Full stops: _____

_____

Question marks: _____

_____

Exclamation marks: _____

_____

Commas: _____

_____

Inverted commas: _____

_____

Apostrophe: _____

_____

Dashes: _____

_____

Brackets: _____

_____

Brilliant Activities for Grammar and Punctuation, Year 5
© Irene Yates and Brilliant Publications

Preposition bank

Word bank of useful prepositions.

about	on		
above	onto		
across	opposite		
over	out of		
after	outside		
against	past		
along	among		
around	round		
at	away		
since	through	because of	before
to	toward	behind	below
under	underneath	beneath	beside
till	until	between	by
down	for	from	in
up	upon	in front of	inside
near	next to	of	off
with	within	without	

Can you think of any more to add?

_____   _____

_____   _____

_____   _____

_____   _____

Search for prepositions in shared texts. Make a display of prepositions, which pupils can refer to.

Assessment checklist

Name	Term		
	1	2	3
Can understand and use the following terminology:			
Modal verb			
Relative pronoun			
Relative clause			
Parenthesis			
Bracket			
Dash			
Cohesion			
Ambiguity			
Understands and is able to:			
Identify and use abstract nouns			
Convert nouns and adjectives into verbs using suffixes			
Alter the meaning of verbs by adding prefixes			
Understand and use relative clauses			
Indicate degrees of possibility using adverbs			
Indicate degrees of possibility using modal verbs			
Use devices to build cohesion within paragraphs			
Use devices to link ideas across paragraphs			
Use brackets to indicate parenthesis			
Use dashes to indicate parenthesis			
Use commas to indicate parenthesis			
Use commas to clarify meaning and avoid ambiguity			
Use hyphens to avoid ambiguity			
Punctuate direct and indirect speech correctly			
Add phrases to sentences to make them more interesting			
Understand the difference between a phrase and a clause			
Identify and use adverbial phrases			
Use apostrophes to show contractions			
Use apostrophes to show possession			
Identify and use similes			

Brilliant Activities for Grammar and Punctuation, Year 5
© Irene Yates and Brilliant Publications

Answers

· ·

Re-cap on nouns (pg 6)
<u>Clothing</u>: gloves, beanie, T-shirt, scarf, socks.
<u>Body</u>: legs, head, shoulder, elbow, toenails.
<u>Sport</u>: swimming, rugby, skiing, running.
<u>Food</u>: bread, apple, chocolate, sandwich.

Verb to noun (pg 8)
intention, description, persuasion, departure.

Nouns to verbs (pg 9)
advertise, purify, centralise, glorify, solidify, pollinate, captivate, liquidate, harden, realise, lengthen, apologise.
advertises, apologises, purify, centralised.

More verbs from nouns and adjectives (pg 10)
invite, enjoy, collect, prepare, darken, classify, sadden, simplify, act.

Nouns and adjectives into verbs (pg 12)
beautify, improvise, clarify, horrified, concentrate, advise, surprised, solidify.

Verb prefix – dis (pg 13)
1. disappear, 2. disbelieve, 3. discontinue, 4. disorganised.
discourage, disentangle, disintegrate, disinterest, disobey, disorientate.

Verb prefix – mis (pg 14)
mishandle, misunderstand, misinform, misspelt.
misjudge, misguided, misshapen, misread, misunderstand, mislead.

Verb prefix – re (pg 15)
1. recapped, 2. recharged, 3. recollect, 4. recreate.

Verbs and nouns (pg 16)

Verb	Noun
admire	admiration
depart	departure
describe	description
exist	existence
inform	information
intend	intention
invent	invention
laugh	laughter
lose	loss
move	movement
perform	performance

permit	permission
persuade	persuasion
please	pleasure
rebel	rebellion
serve	service
settle	settlement
decorate	decoration
enjoy	enjoyment
draw	drawing
prove	proof
behave	behaviour
dream	dreaming

Coping with clauses (pg 18)

More about clauses (pg 19)
Because it was the middle of winter <u>the weather was freezing</u>.
<u>The boys played cricket</u> even though it was very hot.
<u>I can't come out</u> until I've cleaned my room.
<u>The dog kept barking</u> until its owner came to take it for a walk.
The trees <u>we scrumped the apples</u> from were my grandma's.
<u>Josh couldn't play football</u> because he'd left his boots at home.
Before you cross a busy road <u>look both ways</u>.
<u>The bus driver had no idea</u> where I needed to go.

Brackets (pg 25)
Harrif invited his friends (there were six of them) to tea.
Lucy went with Anna (her best friend) and Henry's sister.
They had a lot of stuff to carry (drinks, cards,

presents) and a cake.

The bus went the long way round (there was a flood) and they were late.

Double dashes (pg 26)

The moon-jumping competition – it was going to be great – would start at sundown.

Does anybody know when – or where – it's going to end?

We might need warm things – clothes, waterproofs, trainers – to get it really going.

Lots of talking (pg 28)

Henry groaned. It started in half an hour.

His mum said it was tough and he'd miss the first half if he didn't get a move on!

Henry surveyed the mess in his room. "I'll do it when I get back after the match."

His mum said it wasn't good enough, because he would either forget or not bother at all!

How could he forget he asked – she wouldn't let him!

"No I won't either," she said, "I'll nag you till it's done. You won't get away with it."

Henry said it would be fine and rushed out before she could stop him "Nag, nag, nag!' he muttered under his breath.

Anagrams (pg 30)

flees: feels, glare: large/regal/lager, layer: early/relay, licks: slick, items: times/mites/emits, reprint: printer, hoses: shoes, friend: finder, fringe: finger, grease: agrees, expect: except.

Phrases that describe (pg 33)

The cat <u>with the long fur</u> is mine.

The man <u>with brown shoes</u> is a teacher.

The sail <u>on the windmill</u> was broken.

The house <u>on the corner</u> belongs to my gran.

The girl <u>with the skipping rope</u> is my best friend.

The alien <u>on the bus</u> is unhappy.

Phrases that do the job of an adverb (pg 34)

We're going on holiday <u>next weekend</u>. (when)

The alien came here <u>three weeks ago</u>. (when)

The artist painted <u>with great care</u>. (how)

We put all the toys <u>in the toy box</u>. (where)

She read the story aloud <u>in a very happy way</u>. (how)

The cat had a poor bird <u>in its mouth</u>. (where)

<u>After a while</u> we set out for the park. (when)

We watched TV <u>with the sound off</u>. (how)

Modal verbs (pg 36)

1. will/might, 2. would, 3. will, 4. can/may, 5. will/shall, 6. would, 7. could/must, 8. could/can/will/may/must

Adverbial quiz (pg 37)

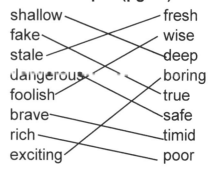

shallow — deep
fake — true
stale — fresh
dangerous — safe
foolish — wise
brave — timid
rich — poor
exciting — boring

Making adjectives (pg 39)

childish, friendly, furry, dangerous, patient, famous, valuable, stormy.

noise, luxury, mercy, play, anger, comfort.

Proper adjectives (pg 40)

China/Chinese, Mexico/Mexican, Switzerland/Swiss, France/French, Scotland/Scottish, Japan/Japanese, America/American, Greece/Greek.

Turkish/Turkey, Dutch/Holland (or The Netherlands), German/Germany, Irish/Ireland, Swedish/Sweden, Egyptian/Egypt, Spanish/Spain, Italian/Italy, Norwegian/Norway.

Comparative adjectives (pg 41)

Positive	Comparative	Superlative
muddy	muddier	muddiest
old	older	oldest
young	younger	youngest
short	shorter	shortest
cold	colder	coldest
small	smaller	smallest
safe	safer	safest
large	larger	largest
wise	wiser	wisest
brave	braver	bravest

Positive	Comparative	Superlative
beautiful	more beautiful	most beautiful
delicious	more delicious	most delicious
honest	more honest	most honest

sorrowful	more sorrowful	most sorrowful
reliable	more reliable	most reliable

Homophones (pg 43)

find – fined, bale – bail, week – weak, witch – which, guest – guessed, hair – hare, pier – peer, poor – pour.

Apostrophes showing contraction (pg 44)

hasn't/ has not, we'll/we will, we've/we have, can't/cannot, o'clock/of the clock, 'tis/it is, didn't/did not, wouldn't/would not.

I am/I'm, you have/you've, I have/I've, who is/who's, I shall/I'll, it is/it's, could not/couldn't, were not/weren't.

We'll go to the park. It's bound to be sunny and it'll be fun on the climbing equipment. You'll need your trainers and maybe some water. Or we'll go to the cafe and they'll serve us some delicious ice-cream!

Apostrophes showing possession (pg 45)

the dog's ears, the farmer's sheep,
the boy's boots, the tiger's tail,
the cats' tails, the library's books,
the sisters' bedrooms, the clock's hands.

Commas (pg 46)

For my birthday, on the tenth, I want all of my friends to come to tea.

The puppy, the one with the waggly tail, might be coming home with us.

My friend Rashid, according to his gran, is the nicest boy ever.

Ian, the best writer in the class, won the first prize for his story.

Lightning Source UK Ltd.
Milton Keynes UK
UKOW07f1146050616

275579UK00002B/11/P